FEAR LESS

SCHOLASTIC

Dedicated to my grandma. Thanks for helping to lift me when I was at my lowest. You taught me confidence, courage and most importantly, you helped me realize that navy really does look good on me.

You will forever be in my heart even when you no longer stand next to me.

Published in the UK by Scholastic Children's Books, 2020
Euston House, 24 Eversholt Street, London, NW1 1DB
A division of Scholastic Limited

London – New York – Toronto – Sydney – Auckland
Mexico City – New Delhi – Hong Kong

Text © Liam Hackett, 2020
Illustrations by Mike Perry © Scholastic, 2020

ISBN 978 14071 9793 7

A CIP catalogue record for this book is available from the British Library.

Printed and bound in the UK by Bell and Bain Ltd, Glasgow
Papers used by Scholastic Children's Books are made
from wood grown in sustainable forests.

1 3 5 7 9 10 8 6 4 2

www.scholastic.co.uk

LIAM HACKETT

FEAR LESS

HOW TO BE YOUR TRUE, CONFIDENT SELF!

SCHOLASTIC

CONTENTS

STAY SAFE!

PLEASE REMEMBER THE GOLDEN RULES OF ONLINE LIFE:

- Think about waiting until you're 13 to use social media.

- Keep your location and personal information **private**.

- Be smart – don't agree to meet face-to-face with an online friend, or send them photos of yourself, until you've spoken to an adult you trust.

- Report anything abusive or that makes you feel uncomfortable to a trusted adult, or you can always speak to Ditch the Label.

- **Remember your digital footprint** – everything you post online is permanent.

LOOK, LET'S BE HONEST.

Growing up is tough. Not only are you expected to do well at everything, but you're also supposed to fit in with everyone else, plus figure out who you are in a scary world that is pulling you in many different directions.

There's pressure coming at you from everywhere. Pressure to perform. Pressure to look a certain way. Pressure to know what you want to do with your life. Just so much pressure and it's normal to feel overwhelmed and confused.

New phone, who this?

Hola! It's a pleasure to meet you. I'm **Liam** and I'm here to help you combat your fears!

Much of the inspiration for this book has come from my own experiences growing up, but also from things that I've learnt as the boss of **Ditch the Label**. If you haven't heard of Ditch the Label, it's a youth charity that helps **thousands** of people each week with everything from bullying to mental health to self-confidence, social media and sexuality.

I launched Ditch the Label – and decided to write this book – because I **really** struggled at school and grew up feeling pretty rubbish about myself. I was never the "stereotypical" guy – I was rubbish at sport, I wasn't interested in cars and I legit had a pet bunny rabbit that I used to push around in a pram **(R.I.P. Sonic the rabbit, this chapter is dedicated to you)**.

THE LOWDOWN ON LIAM

- When I was younger I never knew what I wanted to be but some ideas included a **ghost hunter**, a **gardener**, an **artist** and a **postman!**
- I'm in love with my **PlayStation**
- I ate a live **spider** by accident when I was about five
- I once spoke live in front of **12,000** people at Wembley Stadium
- My favourite meal has got to be a **cheeseburger**
- I have one little brother called Alex and I was nine when he was born. I actually chose his name!

I was bullied for almost **ten years** and didn't have many friends – I walked around on my own most lunch breaks. Like many people, being bullied really affected how I felt about myself and so I had zero self-confidence. I desperately tried to change myself in order to fit in, but nothing seemed to work. Most of the bullying I experienced was name-calling and things posted about me online, but I was also beaten up a few times and once had to have stitches in my face.

By the time I turned fifteen, I struggled to leave the house on my own. I would walk around with my head down hoping that nobody would notice me. One day my **grandma** (hi, Big G!) asked me why I walked with my head down all of the time. I told her it was because I wasn't confident. My grandma said:

"CONFIDENCE IS IN US ALL, BUT SOMETIMES YOU HAVE TO FAKE IT UNTIL YOU MAKE IT." – BIG G

And she was so right!

By the time I left school, I knew that I wanted to create something to help other people and came up with the idea for the charity. After I graduated from university in 2012, Ditch the Label was born.

So, all of the issues in this book are things that I went through growing up and stuff that I now get asked about all the time. I know exactly how it feels to be pressured into being something you're not and I want to share advice that I wish I had been given when I was your age.

Growing up is really scary and I want to do all I can to help you crush those fears to become your true, confident self.

IT'S TIME TO START *your* JOURNEY TO BECOMING FEARLESS.

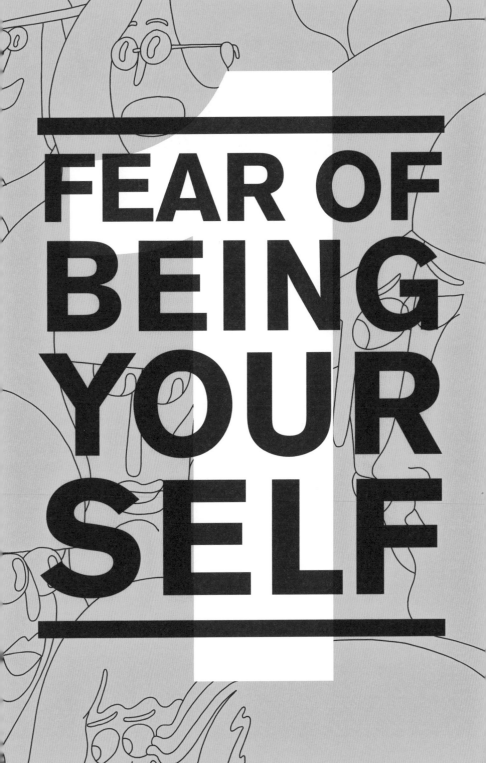

1

FEAR OF BEING YOURSELF

STEREO...
WHAT?

We're going to talk about **stereotypes**. These are the beliefs that pretty much all of us have about other people. Most of the time, these beliefs aren't true.

Sometimes, stereotypes can be **funny** because they are so ridiculous. But they can also be **dangerous** and upsetting – particularly if they are negative.

Hopefully, reading this chapter will help you to smash out of a stereotype and become the **boss** of your own destiny.

BOXED IN

At some point, we've all been labelled and placed inside a box. Whether it's based on gender, race, favourite music, hair colour, hobbies, the clothes you wear or something else, everyone has experienced being boxed in.

Labels **aren't** *always* bad, because they can tell the world an important part of who you are. Sometimes, though, labels come with stereotypes attached to them and often these stereotypes aren't remotely accurate and can be harmful. This can lead to bullying and bad attitudes towards people who are considered different because of their skin colour, disability, sexuality or even their interests and hobbies.

For me, some people didn't think that growing up with a pet bunny called **Sonic** was very "manly" and so I got a few nasty comments – not just from other kids but from grown-ups too. People started to call me a "girl" because I was rubbish at football. Which is silly really, because there are amazing women footballers out there. Because of this I started to wonder why I wasn't like the other boys in my class.

That's just my experience and I know most people have at some point had something similar happen. You may not realize it yet, but by the end of this chapter you probably will.

Grab a pen and draw yourself in the middle of a piece of paper. Draw some boxes around your body and add the labels that people might put onto you. This can be anything from your age to the colour of your skin to how you look. I bet the page is looking a little crowded, huh?

See, we're all put into boxes. I'm going to try and help you to understand why. Plus I'll share some of my top tips on how you can **break free of labels and be truly fearless** when people are putting you under pressure to be someone you're not.

OMG?!

Did you know that a lot of American people think that British people have really bad teeth? Nobody knows for sure why some American people think this, but it may be because an English character in a famous movie from years ago had bad teeth.

Bad teeth aren't the only stereotype held across the world about the Brits. Apparently, British people all know the Queen, live in castles and sit around drinking tea all day!

PINK

OR

BLUE?

PINK

OR

BLUE?

I have a question for you. If you had to choose a new colour for your bedroom walls and it had to be pink or blue, which colour would you go for?

I'm not psychic but there's a good chance that if you are a boy, you chose blue and if you are a girl, you chose pink.

Did you know that you were put into an **invisible box** the second you were born? After a baby's first breath is taken, this box is put around them. And it will go on to affect so many areas of their life, from little things like favourite colour and clothes to the job they'll end up doing, the people they'll be friends with and even things like how often they will cry and the kinds of hobbies and interests they might have.

This invisible box is the first you're ever put inside – and it's all to do with **sex and gender**. Your sex is the **label** (boy or girl) you're given by the doctor at birth, and people generally assume that your gender identity is the same. Of course, we know this isn't always the case: some people may realize their label doesn't fit them and transition from boy to girl or girl to boy, or they may decide that they don't fit either of those labels at all and are non-binary or "agender".

Every culture has an idea of how boys and girls should be, which is called "**gender stereotyping**". There are a ton of gender stereotypes, and in this book I'll talk a lot about them because they affect **everything** we do.

When babies are born, some parents decide to dress them in pink or blue to show whether the baby is a boy or a girl. This is because in the 1940s it was decided that blue is for boys and pink is for girls. This idea is a gender stereotype, and it means that our society assumes that your gender decides what colour your things should be – toys, clothes, bedroom, everything. In fact, you only have to go to a toyshop to see that a lot of it is divided into pink and blue.

These "boy" and "girl" colours actually used to be the other way around – pink was considered manly because it was so loud and vibrant, while blue was calm and feminine. And before that, all babies wore white dresses! I can tell you that it's okay to like blue, pink, both or neither. Your favourite colours have absolutely no relationship to your gender.

These stereotypes are all around us. Let's see how many of them you already know. There are **no** right or wrong answers here, so just stick with the first one that springs to mind.

GINGERBREAD
PEOPLE

Grab a pen and choose some words from the list below. Write them next to which person you think they fit the best on the page opposite.

STRONG | GENTLE | FRIENDLY | PRETTY | EMOTIONAL
RICH | MOODY | CARING | ANGRY | SILLY
APPROACHABLE | LOVING | SUCCESSFUL

Now that you have built two people, choose a job for them from the list below.

PRIME MINISTER | BOSS OF A BUSINESS | SCIENTIST
FOOTBALL PLAYER | NURSE | ARTIST | SINGER | DANCER

Before writing this book, I asked over a **thousand** people to tell me the words and jobs that they would use to best describe both a man and a woman. Now that you have finished both of your characters, let's see how they compare to what I discovered.

MEN

MOODY

STRONG ANGRY RICH

SUCCESSFUL

FOOTBALL PLAYER BOSS OF A BUSINESS

SCIENTIST PRIME MINISTER

WOMEN

EMOTIONAL

FRIENDLY GENTLE

PRETTY SINGER DANCER

ARTIST

APPROACHABLE LOVING

CARING SILLY NURSE

The words and jobs on the opposite page were the most commonly used to describe men and women. What do you think of them? They are quite limiting, aren't they?

Think about who *you* are and what you want to do when you are older. Imagine if you had to choose from one of those four jobs assigned to your gender. Or imagine that when your parents were told if you're a boy or girl, the doctors also had to tell them the kind of job you would have to do when you're grown up!

"THIS IS LIAM, HE'S GOING TO BE STRONG, MOODY, RICH, SUCCESSFUL AND THE BOSS OF A BUSINESS."

It's **hilarious** when put like that, isn't it?!

You may look at the words and jobs and feel like some from both the man and woman groups fit you – and that's okay! If I had to choose some of the words to describe myself, I would probably pick emotional, successful, friendly and boss of a business.

Some of the words and jobs might sound quite funny to begin with. The idea that all women are gentle and all men are moody is kind of lol-worthy. Sure, **some men** are moody but then again, so are **some women** and trust me, if you've ever been on the London Underground or in a busy queue, you'll see that we can all be a little grouchy sometimes.

IN HISTORY

It's always important to understand the history of things, especially when it comes to the rules we're expected to live by. Understanding how these are formed and where they come from can make it easier for us to recognize when we're under pressure and push back when we feel like we're not able to be who we want to be.

Why we're labelled and put into **invisible boxes** can be traced back to the past and the rules handed down to us. These rules are influenced by loads of things, such as outdated science, religion, culture and politics.

Imagine that you're sixteen... Regardless of the kind of job you want to do, you're not allowed to do it. And this is all based on what gender the people around you think you are.

It sounds like **prison**, doesn't it? I honestly can't imagine what that would have been like, but it was the reality for your great-grandparents. Scarily, some countries still impose rules according to gender now.

ASK LIAM

I've always felt different to everyone at school. I'm about to go to secondary school and I'm scared that nobody will like me. What should I do?
Nazima, 10

The truth is you won't be the only one who feels like they don't belong. I can guarantee there will be others in your class who feel the same, but hide it and also hide parts of who they are in order to feel like they fit in.

I always felt like I was different and it was only when I started university that I realized there were plenty of other people out there like me – I just had to find them! My advice is to seek out people who like the same things as you, whether that's through clubs or events, or online once you're old enough to use social media.

Set yourself daily challenges to face the things that scare you – start conversations with new people, join an after-school club and push yourself out of your comfort zone. The more people you meet, the more likely you are to find people who think you're fantastic. Be proud of the things that make you different and know that one day your differences will help you to achieve your dreams.

LIAM X

There we have it – it turns out we've all got invisible boxes around us and with the boxes come rules, which aren't always positive and can make people feel a little … boxed in. So, here are some thoughts from me on how you can break free and be fearlessly

YOU.

We're all told that we should be **"normal"**, but what does that even mean? Normal isn't actually a thing, it's just a word that people use to pressure you into hiding the things that make you special and unique. You weren't born to be "normal" – you were born to be **YOU**!

Always stay true to your **heart** and do the things you enjoy and are interested in the most. You only get one life so make sure you live it for you and not to keep other people happy.

We've all got labels that may explain parts of who we are, but **never let your labels define you**. Remember that stereotypes and rules are a load of hogwash and just because somebody thinks something about you, it doesn't make it true!

Every single person walking the Earth has people that don't like them. The best thing you can do is to rise above it. The more successful you become, the more people will dislike you – mainly because they're jealous of the things you have, your strength, your determination and your **fearlessness**.

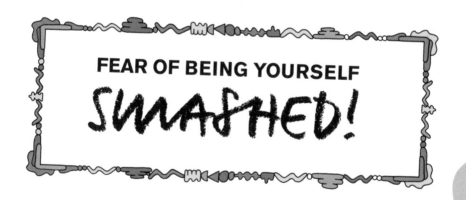

FEAR OF BEING YOURSELF
SMASHED!

P.S.
Sam Renke

Here are some thoughts on dealing with labels, from

ACTRESS AND DISABILITY ACTIVIST.

From the moment I was born, I was stuck with the **negative label** of being disabled. Instead of congratulating my parents on the birth of their beautiful baby girl, I was whisked away to a different hospital and my parents were told to pray for me because I was born with brittle bones (which means my bones are fragile and break easily).

Now that I'm an adult, people regularly tell me that I can't or shouldn't do things because of my disability. I've even had people come up to me to say, **"It's such a shame"** I was born like this. Growing up, I learnt that a lot of people don't fully understand disabilities and quite often can be really mean and rude, sometimes without realizing.

For me, growing up with people constantly telling me I wouldn't achieve my dreams, it made me want to work even harder **to prove them wrong!** And I have to say that every success and achievement I make is made even sweeter because it proves that they *were* wrong.

I USED TO BE ANGRY WHEN PEOPLE SAID THAT I CAN'T DO THINGS, BUT NOW I FOCUS ON LOVING MYSELF AND FACING THE CHALLENGES THAT COME MY WAY.

As an activist, **I use my voice to make the world a fairer and safer place for disabled people** and I love to challenge the often narrow ways in which other people see me.

It hasn't always been easy and some of the labels definitely stuck with me, especially when I was growing up and trying to fit in. But ultimately, nobody has the right to label you as anything, but if they do, my advice is to prove them wrong and instead of letting it beat you down, use it as the thing that drives you **closer to your dreams.**

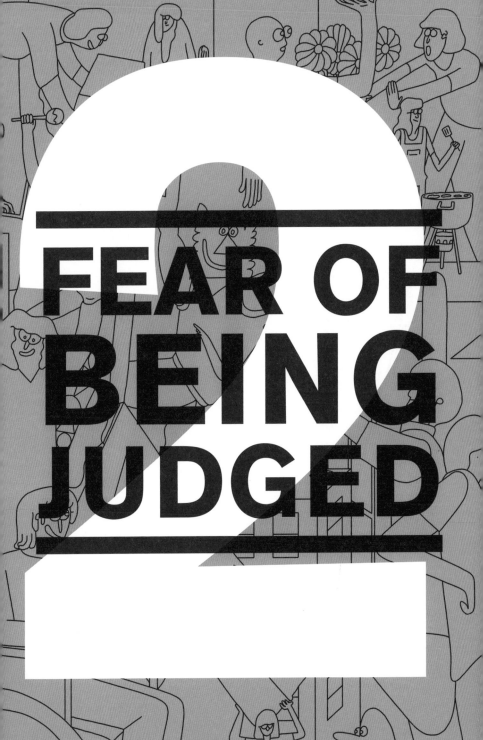

2
FEAR OF BEING JUDGED

CALL IT OUT!

Let's talk about **"unconscious bias"**. It probably sounds really scary but I'm going to tell you all about it and why you shouldn't be afraid to tackle it head-on.

I only learnt about unconscious bias myself a few years ago and I wish I'd known about it when I was younger. I can almost guarantee people will be really impressed if you understand and start calling out unconscious bias when you see it.

As a starting point, take a look at these three questions to see if you know the answers.

 A space rocket carrying five astronauts leaves planet Earth to visit the Moon and the International Space Station, which has no other astronauts inside it. The rocket returns to Earth a month later with six people. How is this possible?

 Katie lives with both of her parents. She's twelve and starts school at 8 a.m. Her mum is at work from 9 a.m. until 5 p.m., so drops Katie off at school on her way into the office. Katie is then picked up every day by her mum at 4 p.m. Can you figure this out?

3 A mum and her son are in a car accident and both are rushed to the hospital. The son needs urgent care but only one nurse is available. The nurse looks at him and gasps, "I can't look after him, he's my son!" But how is this possible?

Here are the answers:

1. **One of the astronauts was female, pregnant and gave birth whilst in space.**
2. **Katie has two mums – they are a couple.**
3. **The nurse is his dad.**

If you didn't get all of the answers, don't worry – most people wouldn't. This is because we all make basic decisions based on the rules our brains have learnt – this is "unconscious bias". A "bias" is when you unfairly prefer something or someone over something or someone else. "Unconscious" means that your brain does it without you even realizing.

WHAT DOES IT ALL MEAN THO?

Right now, your lungs are breathing in **fresh air** – cleaning it, using it to fuel your body and then pumping out all of the stuff it no longer needs in order to keep you alive. Your lungs do this vital job all day, every day and you don't even have to think about it. That's because it happens **unconsciously**.

If it's between pizza and salad for dinner and you really love pizza, you'll be biased towards it and want **everybody** else to choose pizza too.

So, if you stick both of these words together, **unconscious bias** is when our brains decide if we like or dislike somebody without us even being aware it's happening. Did you know it takes less than a second for your brain to make this decision?

Unconscious bias isn't always about people. If there's a pink gift box with unicorns on it and a blue gift box with cars on it, your unconscious bias may make you more likely to go for the pink one if you're a girl and blue if you're a boy. This is because of all the messages your brain has received have taught you this rule and makes your decision pretty much **instant**.

OMG?!

Your unconscious bias doesn't just build stereotypes about people, but about all sorts of things, from places and animals to hobbies and interests. When I was younger, a dog bit me and for about three years afterwards, I was **TERRIFIED** of all dogs. I wouldn't go anywhere near them. This was my unconscious bias keeping me safe. My brain had falsely learnt that all dogs would bite me and created a fear (which I now know wasn't entirely real).

Each and every one of us has an unconscious bias and you may have just seen yours in action with the examples. Yours may have taught you that only men can be astronauts, everybody has a mum and a dad and all nurses have to be women. But now you know that these messages society has sent you aren't always true.

But your unconscious bias isn't always negative and can even keep you safe. For example, if you were walking down the street alone and somebody was walking behind you really quickly, your brain would alert you that there was danger and you would do something to get safe.

HOW DO THESE RULES GET INTO MY BRAIN?

Think of your brain as a hard drive on a computer. Every day, it's sent thousands of messages and it needs to decide, unconsciously, which messages to save and which ones to delete.

Some of the messages will be saved in a folder called **"long-term memories"**, which means you will remember them for a long time. Usually this is something that has made you feel emotional – for example, made you cry, laugh, feel scared or extremely nervous. These will be the memories that you can save and re-open for years and years.

The next folder is called **"short-term memories"** – these are the memories that your brain will save and allow you to remember for a short while.

Then there's your **"temporary"** folder. Here your brain will store files for the next few days and then delete them.

Finally, there's your **"trash"** – the stuff your brain doesn't think you'll need and decides to delete straightaway.

Your brain can move memories from one folder to another and usually it does this when we're learning a new skill. For example, if you watch your first guitar tutorial on YouTube, your brain might decide to store it in Temporary – which is why we're quick to forget when we're learning something new.

After a few more tutorials though, your brain will start to move the memories into your short-term memories folder, and the more often you practise, the more likely it is to go into your long-term memories. If you've ever crammed the night before an exam, chances are you'll remember loads of it the next day but a week later it's all gone. This is why.

Sometimes your brain will merge some of the messages together in order to save space and time. For example, if you go to the supermarket and see a red car and then look around and notice the whole car park is filled with red cars, your brain probably won't remember the first red car you saw. But it will remember that the car park was very red.

The reason I'm telling you all of this is because I think it's important to understand how your brain works before talking about how unconscious bias is built. Remember, your brain does all of this without you even realizing.

Those thousands of messages your brain receives each day? Well some of these messages are about people. They can come from loads of different places like the experiences you have, the things people tell you, the stuff on telly and in films, social media and the Internet, music, adverts on the side of a bus, in the news, the pictures you see… **These messages are everywhere.**

YOU'RE NOW A GREEN PERSON

Imagine that half of humanity has **green** skin and the other half has **blue**.

Imagine that your whole body is green and your family are green too.

You wake up and the news is on TV and there are stories about **a blue person who did something bad**. You walk to school and you see adverts outside shops and on a bus that shows **green people all looking happy**, but **no blue people**.

There are only two blue people at school and **nobody really likes them** and your friend tells you that one of the blue kids did something **bad**.

Your school day finishes and you go home. You're chilling in front of a movie and **all of the goodies are green people but the baddie is a blue person**.

What are some of the messages your brain would have learnt from this day? Let's take a look:

A blue person did something bad enough to be on the morning news.

Green people are happy and good people because of the adverts you saw.

Nobody likes the blue people at school.

Your friend tells you one of the blue people did something wrong.

The movie you watch tells you that green people are the heroes and blue people are the baddies.

Your brain puts these messages together, stores them and starts to learn that blue people are bad and dangerous. So, when you meet a blue person, your brain will instantly tell you to be **scared** and to try and **keep you away from them**.

The truth is, the only difference between green and blue people is their colour. Some green people are good, others are **bad** and it's the **same** with the blue people.

The stories you heard, the news you watched and the movie you enjoyed all sent you these **hidden messages to create an unconscious bias** towards the blue people. What if I now told you that the blue people were cute and cuddly and the green were big goblins? Would your opinion change now that you've got this **new** information?

These conflicting messages and lies happen every day around people of colour. The **unconscious bias** you have about everybody comes from all of the same sources and it's happening every single day. Not all of the messages you see will be good ones and they can lead to a lot of hate and meanness in the world.

ASK LIAM

I feel like sometimes before I even know somebody, I decide that I don't like them and I don't know why. How can I stop?
Tom, 12

You may be relieved to hear that this happens to us all and it's usually for one of two reasons: the first is all about your unconscious bias and how your brain has been programmed by the stories you hear and things you see (think back to the story about the green and blue people, for example).

The second reason could be that the person reminds you of somebody you've had a bad experience with in the past. Whilst it's unlikely you'll have the same negative experience, our brains make shortcuts all the time, which can often lead to mistakes.

My advice is to spend some time getting to know the people you take an instant dislike to and do anything you can to reprogramme your unconscious bias. The top ten tips coming up in this chapter will come in useful to you, so take a look and give them a go!

LIAM X

TEN TOP TIPS

Here's ten top things **you can do right now to train your unconscious bias to be kinder.**

1 **Just knowing** that unconscious bias is a real thing is **a huge positive step forward**, so you're already halfway there. Well done!

2 **Surround yourself with people who are different to you.** Imagine if you had loads of friends who were blue in the previous example, you'd have known that they were just the same as green people and that a lot of the stuff you were hearing was rubbish. You'd have been much less likely to learn the negative stereotypes. Go out of your way to meet people who are in any way different: whether it's skin colour, a disability, sexuality, gender, hobbies and interests.

3 Whenever you think a **negative thought** about somebody or something you see, think a **positive thought** too. Do this every time and you'll train your brain into thinking more positively.

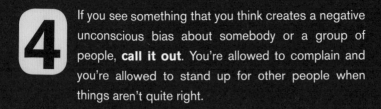

4 If you see something that you think creates a negative unconscious bias about somebody or a group of people, **call it out**. You're allowed to complain and you're allowed to stand up for other people when things aren't quite right.

5 **Educate other people** about unconscious bias! Tell your mates and loved ones, because we all have it and the more people that know about it, the better.

6 **Be fearless!** Don't be afraid to challenge somebody if they make a mean, unfair comment. It's easy to ignore it, but without being challenged, that person may carry on thinking in the same way and it could get worse. Sometimes it might not feel safe to challenge it, and that's okay – report it to an adult instead.

7 If you know that you have a dislike towards a group of people, spend some time with them and seek out **inspirational role models** and positive stories about that group.

8 Whenever you see, hear or think something negative about a person or a group of people, take some time out to **imagine how they would feel** hearing the things that are being said about them. Close your eyes and focus on being positive. Think about something that makes you feel good and think of somebody [you] really love. Once you have the feeling of love in y[our] heart, switch to thinking about the group of people [or] person being attacked and share all of that kindn[ess] and love with them.

9 Most importantly, **don't let your own unconscio[us] bias about yourself hold you back** from do[ing] what you want to. Remind yourself regularly that y[ou] are fearless, you are strong and you can do anythin[g] you put your mind to it.

0 **Remember that everybody is different** and eve[n] if some people look similar, it's always what's on th[e] inside that counts. Turns out the phrase "never jud[ge] a book by its cover" really is true after all.

THINK POSITIVE THOUGHTS!

A lot of the labels I talk about in this book have been built as a result of **unconscious bias** and created from the **thousands of messages your brain receives** each day. I find that training my own unconscious bias to be kinder has made me feel happier and turned me into a better person. Now, whenever I think something negative when I first meet somebody, I think about where those messages have come from and remind myself that they aren't usually true.

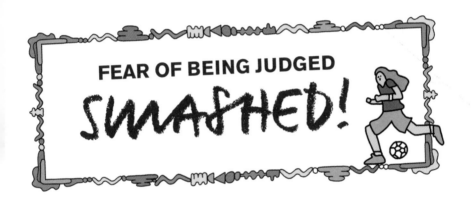

FEAR OF BEING JUDGED SMASHED!

P.S.

Here are some thoughts on dealing with unconscious bias, from

Adam Pearson

DISABILITY RIGHTS CAMPAIGNER, ACTOR AND PRESENTER.

Learning about unconscious bias is really important because it tackles the root causes of many problems such as bullying and hate. Very often, when it comes to bias, we're all just told to change the things we think, without helping people understand where the beliefs come from and without giving them the tools to change the ways in which they think.

I've personally seen so many workshops and training days where people are just told not to be sexist, racist or homophobic and so on, which isn't a bad message but it comes and goes very quickly. You can't reprogramme the ways in which your brain works in just one day – it takes a lot of continuous work and effort.

Unconscious bias training is so much deeper than telling people what to think – it's all about helping people change *how* they think and is something that you do continuously and not just in an hour-long class or training programme.

YOU CAN'T REPROGRAMME THE WAYS IN WHICH YOUR BRAIN WORKS IN JUST ONE DAY – IT TAKES A LOT OF CONTINUOUS WORK AND EFFORT.

FEAR OF NOT FITTING IN

YOU'RE MAGICAL

WHO ARE YOU?

I don't mean your name, how old you are or where you come from. **I mean – *who are you?*** What is it that makes you different to everybody else?

This chapter is all about **personality** – the **magic potion** that makes you, you. Your personality is all of the things that you can't touch or see that make you different (and sometimes similar) to other people.

I like to think of personality as **a recipe that changes from person to person.** Some people share a few of the ingredients, but each and every one of us has a **unique recipe**.

Some of the ingredients that could form a personality include:

- **HOW SHY OR CHATTY SOMEONE IS**
- **THE THINGS SOMEBODY LIKES AND DISLIKES**
- **THE THINGS THAT A PERSON FINDS FUNNY**
- **HOW KIND SOMEONE IS TO OTHERS**
- **IF SOMEONE LIKES TO BREAK RULES OR NOT**
- **HOW ARGUMENTATIVE A PERSON IS**
- **HOW LIKELY A PERSON IS TO BE PRESSURED INTO THINGS BY OTHER PEOPLE**
- **THE AMOUNT OF TIME SOMEBODY LIKES TO SPEND WITH OTHER PEOPLE**

Grab a pen and a piece of paper and try to describe your personality. If you're stuck, choose some of the ingredients from the list above. For some people, knowing their true selves comes easily. But for others, trying to figure out just who they are is terrifying. I want to help you realize that, in a world where you can be anything, **you can be fearless**.

THE SCIENCE-Y BIT

You may or may not have heard of the term **"psychology"**. Psychology is all about understanding people, their personalities, behaviour, thoughts and everything else that goes on in their brains. People can study psychology at college and university to become a psychologist.

For a long time, psychologists have been trying to figure out how to easily describe parts of personalities. To do this, psychologists have developed **personality tests**.

Employers will often ask people to complete such a test when they apply for a job because this will give them an idea as to how well somebody may fit into a workplace and how effective they may be at doing the job they applied for. It is **impossible to measure** someone's entire personality, so these kinds of tests will usually focus on a few key areas – like how shy or chatty somebody is and the kinds of things that make them feel happy and motivated.

Whilst **every personality is unique**, some people may share a few of the ingredients. Psychologists spend a lot of time trying to figure out how people can be grouped together. For example, a psychologist working for a supermarket may create groups of customers who have things in common in order to understand the kinds of things they like to buy, and when and where they like to buy them.

You can't see or touch your personality because scientists believe it's hidden away inside your brain. So, there's still a lot that we don't know about personalities. Some people believe that your personality is part of your soul and when you die, your soul lives on. Other people believe that there's no such thing as a soul and when we die, our personalities also die. There are so many opinions because nobody really knows and scientists haven't fully figured it out.

DO PERSONALITIES CHANGE?

Yes. Psychologists say that our personalities change **as we grow older**.

Which makes sense when you think about it. I couldn't imagine my granny doing the things that I do or being as loud as I am or as interested in sharing her thoughts with the world on social media. She probably would have been similar when she was my age, but her personality and interests have since **changed**.

Who you are today is different to who you were five years ago. Your personality will continue to change as you grow older, because your life will change – you will learn new things and gain more experiences. Some scientists say that your **hormones** not only change your physical body, but your personality too.

OMG?!

Some of the ingredients in your personality are actually hardwired into your DNA and come from your parents! Scientists think that even some of the things you're scared of (spiders, eek!) could come from your parents, too.

Sometimes we have to adapt our personalities to different situations and change how we are, just a little bit. Can you think of any situations where you'd act a little differently to how you normally would?

If you can't think of any, here are some examples:

- When around new people, sometimes we can **act quieter and more shy** than we normally would when with people we know and trust.

- The way we **all behave in school** and at **work** is very different to how we behave at **home** and how we are with our mates at the **weekend.**

- Next time you go to the doctor's, notice how **everybody whispers!** It's really funny and I don't know why, but there's something about a waiting room that makes everyone much more likely to whisper and to **be more private.**

- It's normal for people to be different when they **eat in a restaurant** with loads of people versus when they **eat their evening meal at home** in front of the telly.

- When **playing multiplayer games**, it's common for people to **act a bit braver and more aggressive** than they usually are offline when they're not gaming.

- **When upset about something**, we often have a tendency to withdraw from others and to want to **be alone**. This can make us **appear quieter** than we usually would be.

Also, I don't know about you, but I always **felt really shy on the first day back at school** but would usually feel a bit more **open and be louder towards the end of term.**

There are so many more examples that I could list! Start to think about situations where you or somebody you know changes their personality a little bit in order to adapt to the situation.

Everything I've just described is what psychologists call **"adaptive behaviour"** – we're all programmed to do it in order to fit into new situations.

Adaptive behaviour can often be fun and give you an opportunity to be louder or sillier than you would normally be allowed to. But other times it can feel uncomfortable – like when you're at a birthday party and don't know anyone and feel like you can't truly be yourself, so you hold your personality back.

ASK LIAM

I have a group of mates at school and we usually do stuff at weekends together, too. There are six of us, but I'm closest to one of them and we usually spend time just the two of us without inviting other people.

The only thing is, he acts differently when we're in a group and I don't like him as much as when we're gaming or hanging out just the two of us because he's usually louder and a bit annoying in the group. Why is he like that?
Donnie, 11

This is an example of him using his "adaptive behaviour" and although it's confusing for you, it may actually be a hidden compliment. For whatever reason, it sounds like he needs to change his personality when in the group in order to feel like he belongs and to make people like him more.

The fact that he is calmer and more chill when it's the two of you makes me think that he really feels like he can be himself then. Maybe he's worried that other people are louder and funnier than him and he's scared of being left out?

It sounds like you've got a really decent mate, and he's doing what we all do in order to feel safe. It's likely he'll eventually figure out that he doesn't need to change who he is in order to make people like him, and that he should find people who like him for who he really is. Try not to let it get to you and make sure he knows how much you like spending time with him.

LIAM X

PERSONALITY RULES

Believe it or not, there are a lot of **personality stereotypes** out there that can make it really uncomfortable for somebody if their personality doesn't match the expectation. Sometimes these stereotypes can lead to people making rude comments, or even bullying another person because they are considered different.

But the reality is, we are all different, and we all have our own little things that make us unique. Sometimes these differences can feel like a **weakness**, especially if they attract nasty comments – but in reality, they can be the things that make you **strong**.

Ditch the Label research found that there were a lot of stereotypes about the personalities of men and women. **Women are supposed to be gentle, kind and friendly** and **men are supposed to be strong, bossy and motivated**. These stereotypes would be true if there were just two types of personality, but there are **literally billions**, each unique to every person walking the planet.

A lot of gender stereotypes come from the era where women were expected to stay home and raise children whilst men were expected to work. There was a time when women **weren't allowed to get a job** or to go to **university**. Society put women under pressure to be quiet and to be kind and friendly to all. Meanwhile, men were expected to be **strong and aggressive** and would need to be responsible for bringing home money.

These pressures made both women and men very unhappy, which is why, over time, there have been efforts to make men and **women equal**. We're not fully there though, because these stereotypes still exist. I believe that we can all destroy them by fearlessly being ourselves and not allowing the rude comments of other people to change our personalities.

YOU'RE NOT ALONE

You may be pleased to know that most people feel like the personality rules aren't accurate to them and their personality. Almost half of us have had rude things said or done to us because other people think that we're different.

The reality is, just because you're a girl, it doesn't mean you have to be quiet and kind. Just because you're a boy, it doesn't mean you have to be bossy and aggressive.

ASK LIAM

People always call me bossy and tell me that I'm too loud. There's a boy in my class who is even louder than I am and people think he's really funny and nobody ever says anything mean to him.
Redina, 12

I think a lot of people will understand your situation. Most of us at some point have been told that we're either too loud or too quiet, but the fact is, this part of our personality is pretty much out of our control. And it definitely doesn't change because of your gender!

Some people are extroverted (loud and like to be around a lot of people) and some people are introverted (quiet and prefer to be alone) – and that's okay. My advice is to try and find other people who are like you and spend more time with them.

I like to think of extroverted and introverted as a scale from 1 (introvert) to 10 (extrovert). We're all on the scale somewhere and people are rarely 100 per cent one or the other, I think it's great that you are staying true to who you are. Remember that the problem is with the people making the mean comments, not with you. It's totally fine to be a bossy, extroverted girl!

LIAM X

FINDING YOUR TRIBE

Let's finish this chapter with a really important reminder: **some things can affect your personality, but others cannot.**

Examples of the things that can affect who you are include your experiences, age, hormones, DNA and the people you spend time with.

Things that do **not** determine your personality include your **gender, skin colour, a disability, your sexuality** or **your appearance.**

Sometimes you might be **under pressure** to act a certain way because of what people see when they first look at you, but please know that we all feel that pressure sometimes so you are not alone. Whenever this happens, remind yourself that the problem is the other person and the stereotypes that they believe. **You are never the problem.**

You were made this way and the **thousands of ingredients** used to build your personality cannot be bought – they are unique to just you. You are stronger than you may sometimes believe and you do not need to change for anyone.

I know how tough it is to feel like you don't fit in, but the truth is most people feel the same – some just hide it better than others. Find and surround yourself with people who are like you and don't try to scare you into squeezing inside an invisible box created from **made-up rules**.

REMEMBER

That you are the grandest, most colourful and most fantastic cake and there is nothing wrong with your recipe.

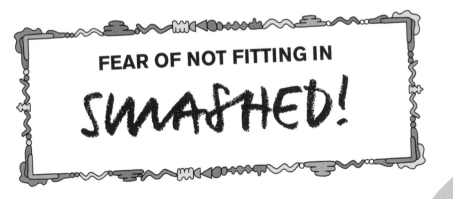

FEAR OF NOT FITTING IN
SMASHED!

I remember there being a certain age when I started to become painfully self-aware. I began to worry that I was "too much" – it was around the age of fifteen and this feeling of "too much-ness" crept in along with that little niggling voice we all know too well which told me to shhh and to try to "blend in". I felt I was either too loud, too emotional, too passionate or too opinionated. I wanted to shrink myself down to fit into the boxes I thought "normal" people fitted into.

It took a little work and a lot of hyping from my friends to help me realize that what I really had was a gift: it meant I could get on a stage and give speeches, make people laugh and share my thoughts with integrity. I had just been looking at it all from the wrong perspective. Instead of being too much, I realized I was enough and that there is definitely no such thing as a "normal person". In truth, the likelihood of you being able to change your personality is nigh on impossible, so be proud of who you are, because there is only one you in the whole world, how amazing is that?!

It's time to start nurturing the longest relationship you will ever have, and that's the one with yourself. Don't waste your precious energy worrying about if people like you – there may be some people that don't, but as long as you like you, that really is all that matters.

SELF-ACCEPTANCE IS A MARATHON AND NOT A SPRINT AND CHANGES DON'T COME OVERNIGHT. TAKE IT DAY BY DAY AND TRY TO FIND ONE THING, NO MATTER HOW SMALL, TO LOVE ABOUT YOURSELF EVERY DAY.

4 FEAR OF YOUR EMOTIONS

EMOTIONS, THEY'RE SCARY

We all have emotions. Some of them are **positive** and make us feel good and others are **negative**, making us feel well … a little down in the dumps.

Our emotions don't just affect how we are feeling – they can often influence our behaviour and personality. When we're stressed, we are more likely to be grouchy and unfriendly. When we're sad, we can feel like we want to be alone or can end up crying. When we're excited, we get a bit sillier than usual and when we're near someone we fancy, it isn't uncommon to be shy and get a serious case of being lost for words (**#awkward**).

Let's explore what emotions actually are, what causes them and what you can do when you're struggling. You may be surprised to know that stereotypes and labels can affect how we choose to display and react to our emotions.

Look at the words below – can you guess which emotions and behaviours are most usually associated with a man or a woman (or both)?

EXCITEMENT ARGUING

NOT TALKING ABOUT YOUR FEELINGS

TALKING ABOUT YOUR FEELINGS

BEING IN LOVE SADNESS

CRYING FIGHTING

HAPPINESS ANGER

BEING SILLY

It's a trick question! We are all capable of experiencing the emotions and behaviours listed above. But stereotypes sometimes make us believe that the **gender** you are can make you more or less likely to experience them. **This is a very dangerous myth.**

Often women are thought to be the most likely to cry and talk about their feelings and men are thought to be angry and the least likely to talk about how they feel. **None of this is true** and it is harmful because it puts us into boxes and can prevent people from dealing with their emotions in healthy ways.

THERE ARE CHEMICALS... IN YOUR BRAIN

The fact is: **our emotions are beyond our control.** They are determined by the chemicals in our brains. The only thing we can control is how our emotions affect our **behaviour** and the things that we do.

Our brains are **ridiculously clever** because they manage our emotions without us even being aware of it. Have you ever felt so angry you've said something you didn't mean? Or have you ever had a rush of energy and excitement when you've done something scary?

These are all examples of our brains **releasing chemicals** into our bodies that make us feel different. There are a ton of chemicals your brain uses – here are **three** you definitely need to meet:

- **Cortisol** is released when you feel stressed.
- **Adrenaline** makes you more alert.
- **Dopamine** (working hand in hand with other hormones) makes you feel happy when it's high but sad when it's low.

LET'S TALK ABOUT
STRESS

Growing up is stressful. It's ~~scary~~ and sometimes it's a total headache. It's made even worse by doing exams, going through drama with your mates, trying to fit in, having to keep your bedroom tidy and having arguments at home.

And that's not even including all the **hormones** and changes your body is going through. Moving schools, moving house, your parents arguing – honestly, there are, like, a million stressful things that I could list here and we probably still wouldn't have listed them all.

If you had to choose **three** of the most stressful things that have ever happened to you, what would they be? If you can't think of the most stressful, think about things that have made you feel stressed lately – **they don't have to be big things.**

Stress comes in all shapes and sizes. You can feel a heavy rush for a short period of time, like if you miss the school bus or have been caught doing something you shouldn't. You can also experience smaller amounts of stress that last for a long time, like if you're worried about starting a new school or you've got exams coming up. The kind of stress you experience is based on the amount of cortisol your brain releases over a certain period of time.

CORTISOL

If you have too much **cortisol** over a long time, it can really start to affect your mood and health. This is why it is important to get rid of cortisol when your body doesn't need it.

ADRENALINE

If you're stressed because of a dangerous or unexpected situation, your brain will release **adrenaline**.

It gives a rush of energy and can trigger your **"fight or flight"** response. This is when you either run away from a stressful situation or stay to battle it. This response was crucial for survival back when humans lived in caves and kept them safe by allowing them to respond quickly to **a dangerous situation** (like being approached by a hungry tiger!).

REMEMBER

You can't control your emotions (which is a scary thought) but you can control how your emotions affect your actions. Understanding what these chemicals are doing in your brain can help you become fearless in the face of emotion.

OUR BRAINS REACT TO THE WORLD AROUND US

Today, it's very unlikely a tiger will ever chase you, but we have new dangers – like busy roads and dark alleyways. Luckily we still have our **fight or flight response** there to keep us safe.

I was once driving on the motorway on holiday in Spain and was feeling pretty relaxed. Suddenly, the car in front started to skid across the road and the driver lost control. My brain released **adrenaline**, which made me super alert and meant that I was able to respond quickly to avoid crashing into the other car. Without the adrenaline, it is likely my reaction would have taken a little longer and could have meant I'd have crashed and been injured. Soon afterwards, I started to feel stressed from the release of **cortisol** and had to pull over for a few minutes to calm down, which helped to reduce my stress levels.

Our brains have become so amazing at controlling the ways in which we react to the world around us by giving us all of these magical emotions. The fact is, even though the labels may suggest otherwise, we all experience every single emotion from deep sadness and fear to happiness and excitement – it doesn't matter who you are or what some of your invisible boxes might be. You should never try to cover up your emotions or pretend that they don't exist, because they do and hiding them away can only make you feel even worse in the future.

FEELING HAPPY
HiGH DOPAMINE

THE HIGHS AND THE LOWS OF DOPAMINE

Dopamine is a chemical that affects how happy or how sad we feel. I like to imagine it as a scale.

Your brain releases dopamine whenever you do something that makes you **feel good**. This changes from person to person, but for me whenever I do something that I enjoy, like exercise, gaming, laughing with friends or listening to music, I feel good!

Can you think of five things that make *you* feel good? Some examples could include:

STROKING YOUR PET | GOING ON AN ADVENTURE
PLAYING SPORT | COOKING | DANCING
BEING IN YOUR FAVOURITE CLASS AT SCHOOL
WATCHING FUNNY VIDEOS | MEDITATING

If you're not doing enough of what you enjoy, then your brain won't release enough dopamine to keep your good mood up. This is when we can start to feel sad. Sadness can also be triggered when something bad happens and in these situations, we can start to feel low and not really very interested in doing the things that make us feel good.

FEELING SAD
LOW DOPAMINE

FEELING MEH...

Regardless of who you are, **feeling sad and low is perfectly normal and healthy**. It's also perfectly normal and healthy to express this emotion! Just because you can't control your emotions doesn't mean that you aren't allowed to express them or try to manage them in a positive way. Don't be afraid to try!

Often people try to **hide** it when they feel sad because they may find it embarrassing or may want everybody to think that their lives are perfect. **The myth that men don't cry or feel sad, only women do, is especially dangerous** – both because it's untrue and also because it can lead to boys and men not dealing with their negative emotions in positive ways.

I want to help you smash the fear of showing and sharing your emotions. **It's okay to cry, no matter who you are.**

If you feel very, very sad and low a lot of the time, it is a good idea to speak with an adult or doctor. Check out the resources page at the end of the book.

OMG?!

The actor Ryan Reynolds grew up feeling some of the pressures you may be feeling. He had three big brothers, his dad was a boxer and worked for the police, and Ryan felt a huge amount of pressure to act a certain way in order to be seen as a "man".

As he grew older, Ryan realized that he didn't have to pretend to be something that he wasn't and learnt that everything he'd been taught about being a man wasn't even true. Now he says that he enjoys having a masculine and a feminine side and being true to himself has been important to him for a long time.

Ryan's story really does show that things are changing and for the better!

YOU'RE A BUCKET!

When I think about my own emotions, I like to imagine a **bucket** tied around my back on my shoulders. It starts off empty, but whenever something makes me feel bad (like stressed, angry or sad), the bucket starts to fill up with sand.

At first, I don't really notice it because it isn't very heavy but then the bucket starts to get heavier and heavier as it becomes filled with **negative emotions**. Eventually, I'm walking around with a huge weight on my shoulders and everything starts to feel uncomfortable and **exhausting**.

Carrying all of this weight around isn't relaxing – in fact, it feels pretty rubbish and only makes all of those negative feelings **even worse**.

The good news is, nobody has to have a bucket of sand tied around their shoulders! **BUT**, negative emotions really can be like carrying around a heavy load: when we ignore and don't deal with them in the right way, they can weigh us down.

Have you ever had that feeling when you've sorted something out that has really played on your mind? Like if you've made up with a friend or resolved an argument? It literally feels like a huge weight has been lifted, doesn't it? That's because you've emptied your invisible bucket! Being aware of what weighs you down and why (the chemicals!) is essential to helping you break free from the stereotypes attached to emotions. This will also help you to be confident in expressing yourself.

When I first started **Ditch the Label**, I wasn't able to go on holiday for a few years. When I eventually went away, I got really sick. I was in Madrid and my throat was that painful, I could hardly talk or swallow. I was there with my friend and I felt so bad because I just wanted to sleep all of the time, so it didn't feel like much of a holiday! When I got home, I did feel like some of the weight I'd been carrying around had been lifted and I now know that the reason I fell ill was because I was stressed for a very long time and hadn't been looking after myself properly.

This isn't uncommon. Research has shown that carrying around a full bucket of negative emotions will not only **damage your mental health**, but it will affect your **physical health** too. Holding in emotions and feeling like you can't cry can actually make you ill – don't fall into the trap, try to be fearless with who you are!

DAILY HACKS FOR DEALING WITH NEGATIVE EMOTIONS

Well, there you have it. Your brain is ridiculously clever at keeping you safe and helping you react to the things that life throws at you. By releasing chemicals, your brain can encourage you to act or behave in a certain way. We've learnt that there isn't much you can do about your emotions, **BUT** you can control how you respond to them.

When something bad happens, you can ignore it and store it in the bucket or you can do something positive to try and deal with it. We know that ignoring and storing will eventually make things worse, so what can you do to stop the bad emotions from holding you back? Here are some of the tricks I've learnt over the years – I hope that they will help you too.

Did you know that **exercise** can reduce the amount of cortisol in your body? Things like boxing, swimming and running are great things to try when you're seeing red.

Grab some old newspapers and **rip them up**, as aggressively as you like. You could also try grabbing a pen and using it to **scribble** all over them beforehand.

Go somewhere and **scream/shout** as loudly as you possibly can. If you can't find anywhere, try doing it into a pillow. This will give you an instant release of anger.

Go for a kick about with a **football**. Kick it against a wall as hard as you can and imagine the wall is the thing making you angry. Just don't go annoying your neighbours!

Write a strongly worded letter to the person who has upset you, saying exactly how you feel and what you think of them. Be as brutally honest as you like and then **destroy the letter** by ripping it up and throwing it away.

Try a "**forgiveness meditation**". Forgiving somebody is one of the most selfish things that you can do because staying angry with them only harms you. You're the one carrying that anger around with you, not them. So don't let them win and remember that forgiveness is your friend.

If you're comfortable doing so, **talk calmly** with the person who has annoyed you. Don't do this when you're still angry because you may end up saying things you'll later regret.

Rant with somebody you trust and **get it all off your chest**. Sharing your problem really does halve it.

Cry. **Let it all out**. A good cry can help release all of the stress hormones in your body, whilst encouraging your brain to release some of that dopamine. Crying is healthy and a quick way to offload some of that weight.

Try a **meditation** – there are loads on YouTube, including tutorials if you've never done it before.

Talk about it with the people you trust and give your loved ones a **cuddle**. Hugs are scientifically proven to make you feel better. Scientists have actually researched the benefits of hugging! That must have been a very happy lab…

Remind yourself of the things you're **grateful** for. I like to keep a gratitude diary and write down three things each day, big or small, which made me feel good.

Sort out your bedroom. Tidy it up and **get rid of some clutter**. You'll be amazed at how much it'll help.

Grab a pen and paper and write down everything that's stressing you out. Below it, come up with a couple of things you can do to help fix the situation and there you have it: your **stress survival plan!**

Write **lists**! This is my favourite thing to do, especially when I've got loads going on. Putting it all into a list makes you feel less pressured and ticking things off feels amazing. Sometimes I'll add things that I've already done, just so I can give them a tick!

Head to the next chapter and read all about **"the flow"** and **do something** that makes you feel yours.

REMEMBER

Emotions are normal and everyone experiences them. Every single person is capable of crying or being so angry they shout. **Stereotypes** you see on telly and in films, for example, might make you believe otherwise, but remember that those stereotypes are false. Hiding your emotions away and pretending that they don't exist will not help, so take the pressure off yourself and don't let anybody else push you into being an **emotionless robot**.

Check out the Useful Resources (page 148) for some really awesome places where you can go to for help and support when you're feeling low.

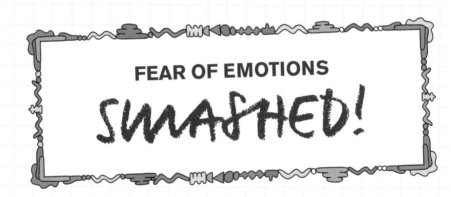

FEAR OF EMOTIONS
SMASHED!

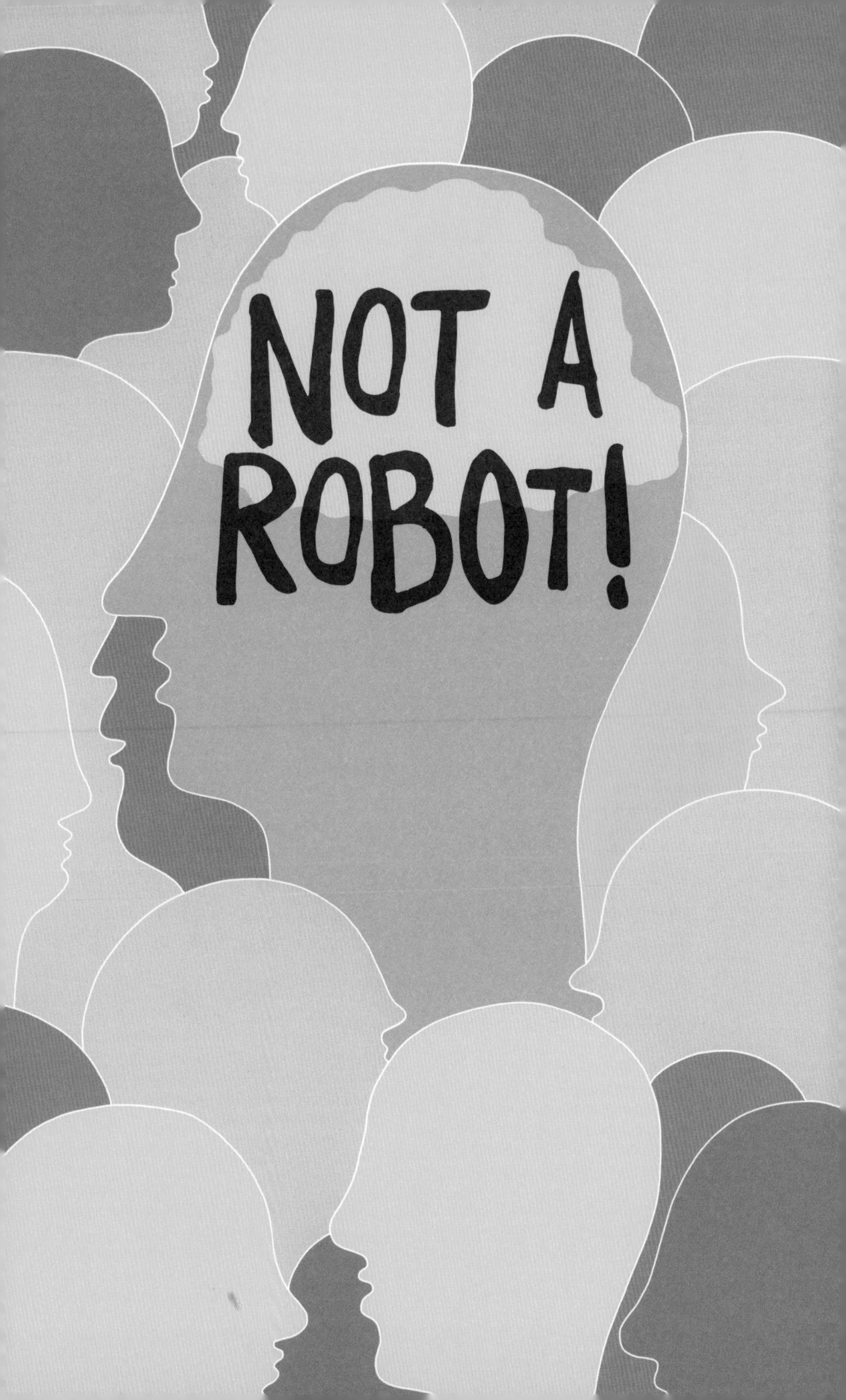
NOT A
ROBOT!

P.S.
Jacob Blyth

PROFESSIONAL FOOTBALLER

I think it's important to always know that you're never alone when it comes to dealing with the negative stuff. There are always people who are going through worse things and I think it's important to remind myself regularly and often about the positives – even things you don't usually think about, like having a roof over your head, people that love and care about you, decent food in the cupboard, all the things we take for granted.

It's normal to feel negative emotions – we all go through them. I think a lot of men are put under pressure to hide it and to not talk about their feelings, but I disagree – I don't think that's healthy and talking about it always makes things so much better. A problem shared is literally a problem halved so I find talking helps me a lot.

REMEMBER THAT WE ALL GO THROUGH STUFF; IT'S WHAT MAKES US HUMAN.

FEAR OF EXPRESSING YOUR SELF

MY GARDEN HAS A SECRET

If you go outside and look at my garden, one of the first things you'll notice is how perfect my grass looks. It's a lush green, perfectly cut and looks the same all year round. But my grass has **a deep, dark secret ...** nobody knows this, so please keep it to yourself ... but it isn't real grass. **It's 100% fake.**

I chose the fake stuff because I'm too lazy to get the lawn mower out every few weeks. Instead, I just hoover it every now and again. Thinking about it, my neighbours probably think there's something wrong with me whenever they hear the sound of a hoover coming from the back garden, but at least I don't have to clean out a lawn mower, so who's laughing now?!

Look beyond my fake grass, and nestled in the flowerbeds you'll spot a few weeds, a couple of trees and a handful of flowers. My garden looks okay but I can't really be bothered with it. I like it because it's low maintenance and I don't have to give it too much love in order for it to look good. This is my first house with a proper back garden and I do enjoy having it, mainly because it attracts a ton of wildlife – loads of birds, a couple of frogs and a cheeky cat from next door, who keeps on going to the loo on my fake grass. (I'm less fussed about the cat to be honest, but still.) It's nice to sit out in the garden on a sunny day and relax for a while, but it isn't somewhere I'd choose to spend *all* of my spare time.

Let's rewind a little bit and go back to eight-year-old Liam. My whole life was gardening. I used to watch all of the gardening shows on TV and would sit around drawing pictures of my ideal garden – they'd usually have a big water feature, loads of greenery, flowerbeds and a couple of trees. I loved gardening that much, I managed to convince my teacher at school to set up a miniature gardening club. It was only me and maybe a couple of others who ever went, but I couldn't get enough of it. We used to create tiny gardens, no bigger than 30 centimetres wide, from soil, moss, stones and doll-sized figurines.

I used to daydream about how I'd like my garden to look when I grew older and had a big scrapbook I used for gardening inspiration. I tried to convince my mum to install a pond in the back garden, but Alex had just been born and she said it probably wasn't the best idea. I was gutted! My hero at the time was Alan Titchmarsh – a then 50-year-old guy who presented my favourite gardening show, *Ground Force*. I **never** missed an episode.

Although gardening wasn't a typical hobby for someone my age, it was something that really gave me a thrill and something that I felt excited about. People would sometimes make mean comments and try to encourage me to like something different, but I pushed back and ignored them.

Unfortunately, like most things, stereotypes can affect the kinds of interests and hobbies you have and I wanted to include this chapter to encourage you to break free and do the things **YOU** want to do and not the things you may feel pressured into.

R.I.P. GROUND FORCE

Over time, my interests started to **change** and I started to spend my time doing other things. Eventually I stopped watching *Ground Force* and my gardening scrapbook went to the hobby graveyard, aka the bin. Present-day – you guessed it with my fake grass – I'm **not** really that interested in gardening.

As I grew older, like most people, my hobbies and interests changed. Now they include things like fitness, gaming, writing, design and business. Some people manage to find a job that fits in with their interests and hobbies and others like to keep work and personal life separate. For me, it's a bit of both and I personally believe that doing something you really enjoy and getting paid for it is the **absolute dream**.

By now, you've probably guessed that this chapter is about **interests and hobbies**. And you've probably got some of your own – things you like to do in your spare time when you're not at school or doing all that homework.

Your interests include the things you like to watch, read, learn about or listen to … so anything from your favourite subject at school, to the music you listen to and your favourite channel on YouTube. Your hobbies are the things you like to do; things like swimming, painting, singing or learning to code. Something can both be an interest and a hobby and most things usually are. For example, you might be really interested in dancing, so follow famous dancers online and watch online tutorials but then also dance at a class.

HOBBIES ARE GOOD FOR YOU

It's really important to have interests and hobbies that excite you – it can be good for your health! Doing things that give you **good vibes** is a great way of boosting the feel-good chemical we spoke about earlier, dopamine. I like to go on my PlayStation when work is really busy and I feel stressed. Gaming for a couple of hours helps me to **relax and unwind**, which means that by the next day, my stress levels have decreased and I feel like me again. I also aim to go to the gym on my lunch break – I've found that it makes me happier and more productive in the afternoon because exercise makes you feel good and helps **get rid of stress**.

Have you ever been doing something that you enjoy so much, you've actually lost track of time? Hours could have gone by but you feel like you've only been doing it for a few minutes. Psychologists call this the **"flow"** – it's when you find something that you enjoy so much that it completely takes over your mind. People find their **"flow"** in different ways – from playing sport and games to graphic design and composing music. Psychologists say that doing things that give you flow makes you happier, healthier and feeling better about yourself.

Grab a piece of paper and make a note of the last time you experienced flow and have a think about how you could experience it more often. If you're struggling or don't remember when you last experienced it, don't worry – there's loads of ideas online, just search for things like "activities for flow" and "hobby ideas".

WHERE DO MY INTERESTS COME FROM?

Psychologists don't fully know the answer – some say you're born with your interests and others say it comes from the world you live in and the experiences you have. I personally believe it's a bit of both and very similar to how your personality is built (flick back to Chapter 3).

We're all excited by different things, which is why there are millions of different interests and hobbies! Some are more popular than others – an interest in Ariana Grande is probably more popular than an interest in collecting stamps – but really it is all about whatever makes you **feel happy**.

Have you ever got really excited when you found out someone else likes the same Netflix series as you? Or plays the same game? Or follows the same YouTuber? I love that moment when you realize you've got something in common with somebody. It's really important to make sure you have people in your life who share some of the same interests, because it's great to talk about and do them together.

DO STEREOTYPES
AFFECT INTERESTS AND
HOBBIES TOO?

In short, yes. And it may be more common than you think. Four in ten people aged thirteen to twenty-five who have experienced bullying said it was because somebody targeted them over their interests or hobbies.

Look at the list below – which hobbies would you say are for a man, which for a woman and which for both?

MAKE-UP **SWIMMING**

HORSE RIDING **ICE-SKATING** **DRAMA CLASS**

X FACTOR **DANCING** **BALLET**

BASKETBALL **FOOTBALL**

PLAYING GUITAR **FASHION** **GAMING**

ARIANA GRANDE **STAMP COLLECTING**

STORMZY

Hopefully you've guessed by now – it's another trick question.

Anyone can enjoy all of the interests and hobbies in the list. It's just that gender stereotypes tell us this isn't true. Some of those stereotypes come from history, but others come from TV, movies, social media and even the toys you played with as a toddler.

If movies show only women horse riding, it could make men feel like they aren't allowed to do it. If YouTube only shows guys gaming, you guessed it, it makes women feel like they aren't allowed to either. These messages are all around us.

There's a really famous film called *Billy Elliot*, which is all about a guy who wants to go to ballet class. But his parents aren't that into it and he gets a lot of criticism for going. Anyway, he goes and turns out he's an absolute boss at it and ends up becoming a super successful ballet dancer. If he'd listened to what people said, he'd have never have achieved such success and happiness.

If you're looking for some inspiration, there are loads of amazing stories out there and a ton of influencers and celebrities who are following their dreams and interests despite what other people think. It's all about doing the things that make **YOU** happy, and not what keeps everybody else happy.

There are **thousands** of different hobbies and interests out there, the possibilities of how you could spend your spare time are endless. In this chapter, we've seen that stereotypes, once again, aren't really true and can hold people back and also that having some decent hobbies can be good for you.

ASK LIAM

I want to start going to drama class after school but my mates say I'm a girl because of it. I have always wanted to give it a try. What should I do?
Tyrece, 12

Well, I mean if you are a boy, then you are a boy – regardless of what kind of things you enjoy doing in your spare time! So it sounds like your mates need to hold up with their stereotypes a little! My advice is to lend them your copy of this book once you're done with it and to give drama class a try! Remember that you don't need their permission to do it.

The gender stereotypes all around us make some people believe that certain hobbies are for girls and others are for boys, but it really isn't true. Ask them who their favourite actors are – half of them are likely to be guys, who might have done drama.

Whenever you feel low or like it's something you shouldn't try, have a look at some of the movie/telly actors you admire and remember that like you, they had to start somewhere. They were fearless and ignored the comments of others and just went for it. You too, are fearless and I think your mates secretly might want to give it a try too.

Go get 'em!

LIAM X

TEN TOP TIPS

Want to try something new but worried about what other people might say? Or perhaps you're keeping your hobby a secret from somebody? Here are my top ten tips on how you can be **truly fearless** when it comes to **expressing yourself**:

1 Sometimes we try something and we're not that into it, but other times we may surprise ourselves and find our flow, so try new things – even if you're scared of what other people may think.

2 We're all scared of not being very good at something new, but remember that **EVERYBODY** has to start somewhere. When I played Fortnite for the first time, I was scared and tbh I died straightaway. After a few goes, I managed to come eighth out of a hundred players.

3 If something doesn't give you the flow, know that it's okay to move on. Sometimes people might put you under pressure to do something, but it's okay to say **no** if you don't enjoy it.

4 If people make mean comments, always remember that they may be unhappy with themselves, or may secretly want to try something new but are scared of what other people may think. Try to ignore it and don't let their comments **deter** you.

5 **Surround yourself** with people who like the same things as you. You can meet them in classes, groups and even talk to people online. I'm not going to lecture you about online safety, but never meet an online buddy without a trusted adult present.

6 Use the Internet to find **role models** of the people you admire who have a similar interest or hobby. YouTube is also an amazing place to learn new things and to watch tutorials for free.

7 Research and remember the stories of people who have turned their interests and hobbies into a really **successful and happy job!**

8 Sometimes people might have interests that you think are **silly or weird**, but it's important to remember that other people might think the same about yours. We're all different and it's good for everybody to do the things that they enjoy.

9 **Don't forget** – your interests are specific to you, not your gender!

10 Above all, always remember that you're living your life for **YOU**. Some people might not want to see you happy and enjoying the things you like, but that's their problem, not yours. Let them be unhappy watching you enjoy yourself. **GO. FOR. IT!**

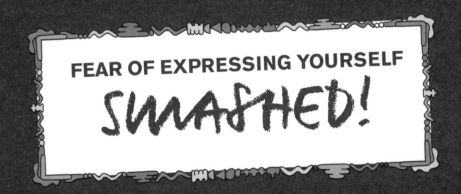

FEAR OF EXPRESSING YOURSELF
SMASHED!

P.S.
Jake Graf

TRANSGENDER WRITER, ACTOR AND DIRECTOR

I don't have a lot of spare time, but when I do, it's usually spent gardening or decorating cakes. I've always loved watching things grow, and can spend hours pottering around in a garden, pruning and chatting to my plants.

As for baking, I spent years creating models out of plasticine and Fimo, so it just seemed like a logical progression to start sculpting things out of fondant, sugar paste and chocolate. To be honest, I enjoy decorating the cake much more than I enjoy baking it, so they sometimes look more impressive than they taste!

When I was little I loved dressing up as characters that I'd made up in my head, always boys or men as everyone was telling me that I couldn't be one in "real life". I know that at the time my parents just thought I was being silly, but really it was helping me get through a very difficult time in my life by pretending to be someone else.

I think that there is a worrying lack of originality these days, with everyone following the herd and trying to fit in. If you have a hobby that you love that makes you stand out a bit, then great! That may be something you end up doing when you're older or may just remain as a much-loved pastime.

DON'T LET ANYONE TELL YOU THAT WHAT YOU'RE DOING IS WRONG - IT'S REALLY NONE OF THEIR BUSINESS.

It will make you much happier in the end, and remember that they're probably just jealous that they're not as original, unique and interesting as you are!

6

FEAR OF BEING A FAILURE

WHAT DO YOU WANT TO DO WITH YOUR LIFE?

This is something **I'm sure you get asked all the time**. When I was younger, I changed my mind constantly and when I said I once wanted to be a ghost hunter, I honestly wasn't kidding!

It was only when I turned sixteen that I realized I was really interested in a career in business. I still didn't fully know what I wanted to do next, so went to study business at university.

I'd always had the idea of Ditch the Label in my head so decided just to go for it. I have been super lucky to find the right job for me – but it took years to figure it out! I have some adult friends who are still trying to decide, and that's okay!

CHANGING YOUR MIND

You're allowed to **switch direction** in life and try new things. When I was younger, I had no idea that I would go on to write a book. In fact, writing was at the bottom of the list. But when I turned twenty-six, I suddenly felt like I wanted to write and then I had the opportunity to put together this book for you.

We've moved on from the days of coal mines and full-time housekeeping. In an ideal world everyone would have the chance to try enough different jobs until they find the one that suits them best. This isn't always easy to achieve but it's worth fighting for, if you can.

I believe that doing a job involving the things you enjoy is so important. I find my job as the boss of Ditch the Label really exciting and I love going into work every day. Sometimes people do jobs that they don't love, either because they have to for a short while or because they were **pressured into doing it**.

My mum worked in a shop for a long time and was really unhappy. She went to work to pay the bills but didn't enjoy it. One day she'd had enough and decided to go to university for the first time. I was fifteen and my little brother was six and it was just the three of us. She really struggled for three years as we didn't have much money but said that graduating at thirty-six was one of the proudest moments of her life. She then got her dream job as a social worker, which was something she always wanted to do but hadn't really known how to get there. Just goes to show it really is **never too late to change your mind!**

Caroline told me that it has become easier over the years, but when she first started out, men would try to make her look stupid when she would take part in debates. There was also no support for her as a new mother – she had had a baby just before she was elected.

The advice from Caroline is to remember that society has come a long way and that **anyone** can do anything! People once believed that women could not be politicians – now they know that they can, and they do it just as well as men.

"Don't let a **fear of failure** or people telling you that you're wrong put you off. We'll always experience failure and it's okay to try something else if it doesn't work out," says Caroline.

HOW AARON BECAME FEARLESS

When he was just thirteen, **Aaron Renfree** shot to fame as one of eight members of S Club Juniors, a pop band launched in 2001. After the band broke up in 2004, Aaron went on to pursue his passion in dancing and is now at the top of his game.

He has danced professionally around the world for the likes of Taylor Swift, Little Mix and The X Factor tour. As one of the only guys in his school learning to dance, Aaron told me he experienced bullying and rude comments from people who didn't understand why he, a boy, wanted to do something that was considered something that only girls were allowed to do. In order to avoid the negativity of others, Aaron tried football, swimming and karate but none of them gave him the same buzz as dancing did.

Things started to change when Aaron met a dance choreographer whilst filming for S Club Juniors. The choreographer told him that he could build a successful life as a dancer and recommended a dancing school in London, where Aaron eventually studied.

Aaron told me that being around other dancers really helped build his confidence – after all of those years, he was finally around people who supported him and wanted him to succeed in dance. After graduating, he started to get his first jobs in the West End and now says that he's so glad he stuck it out and didn't give in to the mean things people used to say to him.

His advice to you is to **never give up** on your dreams. There's so much out there in the world so go and explore it, stick to something you love and don't let people put you down. Focus on school, try to enjoy it and don't be afraid to use the support around you.

IN HISTORY

Back in the olden days *(like way, way, way before the Internet)*, not only were women put off from going to work, but they weren't allowed to **vote in elections** and it was considered unusual for a woman to own and drive a car.

Aside from jobs in mining, men were the main **breadwinners**. So the men would often work manual labour jobs and also did all of the political, legal and "intelligent" work in things like science, maths and engineering.

This history is where some of the **negative stereotypes** we have today come from. Believe it or not, some people still believe that women are better at cleaning, cooking, teaching and nursing and men are better at being lawyers, bosses and politicians.

The fact is, your gender actually makes no difference to your ability to do any of those jobs and you need to find something that suits you, not other people.

There has always been a dangerous idea that all men are strong, in control and intelligent and all women are gentle, caring and less able to work the more physically demanding jobs. These stereotypes are really harmful and absolutely not true.

It was once **impossible** for a woman to study at university. This meant that women could not work the higher-skilled jobs because they were not allowed to get degrees. Men were the only ones encouraged to gain these skills, which forced them into particular roles.

What if a man had wanted to be a ballet dancer? Something considered quite feminine. This would have been pretty much impossible in the past. We have come a long way, but knowing the history of stereotypes can help to explain why some jobs are considered better suited to a man or a woman.

BRAIN SCIENCE

Science tells us that whilst male and female brains are slightly different, those differences do not mean women are incapable of studying at university or that men are incapable of being stay-at-home parents. There is literally nothing, other than the pressure to conform to harmful stereotypes, that makes any of the jobs listed on page 104 impossible for a man or a woman to do.

These stereotypes are sometimes backed up by the titles of jobs. Can you think of any jobs that have "**man**" or "**woman**", or anything else that **implies gender** in the title?

Here are a few I could think of:

- Postman
- Policeman
- Lollipop lady
- Dinner lady
- Businessman
- Midwife
- Chairman
- Fireman

I know it might seem like a small thing, but this language really does feed the negative gender stereotypes. This is why it is important to start taking the man/woman out of job titles.

Here are some examples of change:

POSTMAN → POST PERSON
POLICEMAN → POLICE OFFICER
LOLLIPOP LADY → LOLLIPOP PERSON
DINNER LADY → DINNER STAFF
BUSINESSMAN → BUSINESSPERSON
MIDWIFE → BIRTHING NURSE
CHAIRMAN → CHAIRPERSON
FIREMAN → FIREFIGHTER

BUT I STILL DON'T KNOW WHAT TO DO WITH MY LIFE!

So, how do you choose the right path in life?

Historically, this might have been chosen for you by your family and teachers and most likely influenced by **fake rules in society**. Sometimes this still happens – we all experience pressure from friends, family, teachers and the kinds of people we see who are already in the jobs we dream about.

I believe that it's important to keep an open mind when it comes to careers. After all, the kind of job you decide on might be what you spend the rest of your life doing – so it's **hugely important** that you try to find something you really love. Although you most probably can't get a job eating sweets all day, no matter how much you **love** doing it.

My advice is to start with the things that you enjoy the most. **Research** them to see what kind of jobs they might lead to. If you're not yet ready to decide, please don't feel under pressure – that's okay.

As you start to figure out the things you really enjoy, think about what you are good at and the subjects you like most at school. Don't let what other people might think or say limit your options. You can do anything you want to if you put your mind to it. **But remember** that you might change your mind – that's also okay!

We're all under pressure from other people to do things that we sometimes don't want to. We're also under pressure to be the best and do better than everybody else. But in reality, you have to do what makes you happy and **you're only in competition with yourself.**

OMG?!

Some of the most successful and famous people in the world are those who have fought against the **pressure** society puts them under and gone on to achieve amazing things. Here are some of my favourites:

- **Giorgio Armani** founded one of the biggest global fashion brands, Armani. He started out in the world of medicine but decided it wasn't for him and forged a career in fashion instead.

- **Ellen Degeneres**, a famous TV host in America, started out as a waitress before breaking into the world of comedy and landing her own TV show.

- The founder of BuzzFeed, **Jonah Peretti**, started his working life as a schoolteacher but then quit and launched what is now one of the most popular websites in the world.

- **Vera Wang**, one of the most famous clothes designers in the world, was an editor for a big fashion magazine first, before going on to build her own fashion empire.

YOU GOT THIS.

I don't know about you but I'm feeling pretty inspired right now. I want you to know that you can achieve anything if you put your mind to it. It doesn't matter what gender you are, how much money your family has or what everyone around you says and thinks.

As you grow up, people will never be too shy about sharing their opinions of what you should be doing with your life and what kind of person you should be. I'm here to tell you that you should **live your life for you**. Be a kind and caring person and do the things that you enjoy the most. If other people have a problem with it, that might be because they are unhappy themselves and feel under pressure to change. **That isn't your problem.**

So, whether you're heading for a career in football or nursing, be fearless and don't let the opinions of other people scare you! **You've got this.**

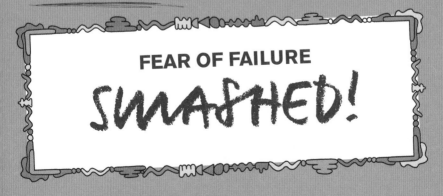

FEAR OF FAILURE
SMASHED!

P.S.
VICKI
SHOTBOLT

Here are some thoughts on life choices from

FOUNDER OF WEBSITE, PARENT ZONE

I had no idea what I wanted to do when I finished my education. Earning some money and being independent were my two biggest considerations and both of those were linked to my main interest at the time, which was partying!

It was only after a couple of jobs I hated that I started to find my ambition. I discovered I enjoyed making a difference and being successful at what I did and by the time I was thirty I knew I was going to run my own social enterprise. Even though social enterprise wasn't really a thing twenty years ago! I wanted to combine being a successful businessperson with making a positive social impact. If I'm very honest, deciding what social issue I was going to focus on came second and took a while to emerge.

MY ADVICE TO ANYONE THINKING ABOUT THEIR CAREER IS TO REMEMBER THAT IT IS A CAREER AND NOT A ONE-OFF OPPORTUNITY.

You have lots of time to find your strengths and if you make the wrong choice to begin with, you can always change your mind.

The main thing is to work hard because no one builds a great career by not trying hard. If your job is to take the notes at a meeting, make them the best notes anyone has ever seen. If you're asked to do something that isn't technically in your role, smash it – because you'll learn with every new challenge and one day your future path will present itself to you.

FEAR OF NOT BEING GOOD ENOUGH

MIRROR, MIRROR, ON THE WALL...

When you woke up this morning and looked at yourself in the mirror, how did you feel about the **reflection** looking back at you? Your response to this question will most likely change depending on how old you are. Generally, people start to feel **worse** about their appearance as they grow **older**, but why is that?

Let's explore where some of these **pressures** come from and talk about ways in which you can feel comfortable in your own skin, no matter what anybody else thinks or says.

This chapter is really **important** to me because, like pretty much everybody, I've really struggled with my own appearance, especially when I was growing up. I first started to feel rubbish about myself when I was in Year 7, after a Year 9 at school punched me and gave me a black eye – two days before our first high school photo. **Not ideal.** I saw around me that I wasn't the only one struggling with how I looked. Even as a grown-up, I still see how bad these pressures make a lot of people feel.

I don't know about you but I think the world would be pretty dull if everybody looked the same.

I love the fact that we're all unique, but there are people and companies out there who unfortunately want to stamp all over our **uniqueness** in order to either make themselves feel better or to make a bit of money.

YOU ARE GOOD ENOUGH AND YOU'LL ALWAYS BE GOOD ENOUGH

The reality is that at some point, you will see or hear something that will make you feel like you **aren't good enough**. It could be an advert on telly, a pic on social media or a really rude comment made by somebody at school. All of these things mount up and build pressure in our minds.

We all experience this – it doesn't matter who you are, how many followers you have, how much money you've got or what you look like. There are no exceptions.

Let me remind you that you are **equal** to everybody else on this planet and **nobody is better or worse than you**. You are good enough and you will always be good enough. Without you, something would be missing in the world and nobody else could

ever replace that. This is true for all of us. We're all meant to be here and sometimes difficult things happen, but everything will always be okay.

In this chapter, we'll be talking a lot about "beauty ideals". These are the pressures that we're all put under by companies and other people to look a certain way. **Beauty ideals** change over time, but also depend on things like the country you're from, your gender and how old you are.

Beauty ideals are all around you, from the toys you play with, to the ads you see on telly. Take a moment to think about a time

when someone or something made you feel like you weren't good enough and made you want to change how you look.

I grew up with the pressure to have clear skin because of the models I saw on TV and in magazines. Today, I'm under pressure to have muscles because whenever I open a social media app, I'm usually blasted with photos of guys who look like an **Action Man figure**. I see the same body shape in so many different places throughout my day – on billboards, TV, magazine ads … **everywhere**. Sometimes the ads get me down because I naturally don't look like that, and I have to remind myself often that **I'm perfect just as I am**.

BEAUTY IDEALS

ACROSS HISTORY

now that we know what **beauty ideals** are, let's look at how [the]y may have changed throughout history. Some of the beauty [ide]als from 200 years ago would be considered absolutely [ridi]culous today. Here's a **quick quiz!**

[Wh]ich of the following do you think are true?

1. It was once considered fashionable and aspirational to be overweight and people were called names for being too skinny.

2. In the eighteenth century, most people aspired to have pale skin and a tan was something to be ashamed of.

3. Back in the days of the Tudors, the **blacker your teeth**, the more attractive you were.

f you answered yes to any of the above, congratulations, because you're right! In fact, they're **all correct**. Let me explain.

Back in the 1700s, being overweight was considered to be incredibly desirable and was a symbol of wealth. It told the world that you had enough money to eat in excess and it was considered fashionable to showcase a bit of extra weight.

Also in the eighteenth century, way before aeroplanes and sunny holidays abroad existed, it was thought that the paler your skin, the wealthier you were; as having a tan meant that you spent a lot of time outdoors doing manual labour – like farming crops or building houses. This was also a much darker time in British history, as racism was prevalent and people of colour were treated terribly, so this also fed into the desire to be pale-skinned.

Back in Tudor times (1485–1603), sugar was really expensive because it came from the East and West Indies. The only way to get it to England was on a boat, which took a long, long time. Sometimes the boats sank or were stolen by pirates, which made sugar even harder to get. This meant that only the super wealthy were able to get their hands on it. In fact, it is **rumoured** that Queen Elizabeth I used to brush her teeth with **sugar!**

Teeth blackened by decay were therefore a symbol of wealth and something people actually aspired to. If you want to recreate this gorgeous look, grab a jar of chocolate spread and a spoon and put some of it on your teeth. You'll soon see how ridiculous it looks. Back then, it was considered stunning. Thankfully this beauty standard no longer exists, as I'm pretty sure your dentist wouldn't be very happy…

BEAUTY IDEALS NOW!

These historic trends really are quite unbelievable by today's standards, but that's only because the beauty ideals have changed. Think about some of the ideals that currently exist. If you're struggling, you could try flicking through a magazine with loads of adverts in, or you could interview family members and ask them what they think.

Grab a pen and paper and note down:

THREE IDEALS
THAT AFFECT EVERYBODY
(for example: having clear skin)

THREE IDEALS
THAT AFFECT MEN ONLY
(for example: having hairy legs)

THREE IDEALS
THAT AFFECT WOMEN ONLY
(for example: shaving your armpits)

THE PRESSURE TO LOOK DIFFERENT

So, why are we talking about this?

Ditch the Label asked thousands of people how they felt about their appearance. One in two said that they would change something if they could. Some people said that they would even consider having an operation in order to feel better about themselves.

We're all under the same beauty ideal pressures and these vary depending on your **gender**. Hopefully, by the end of this chapter, you'll understand the secrets of the people and companies who want to make **you feel terrible** about yourself and ultimately, you'll be able to fearlessly make your own decisions about your body and feel comfortable in your own skin.

MUSCLY OR SKINNY?

Let's look at another list. Which of the following beauty ideals do you think are **specific** to **men**, to **women** or to **both**?

TATTOOS **MUSCLES**

PIERCED EARS **LONG HAIR** **CLEAR SKIN**

SKINNY **HAIRY** **CURVY**

SHORT SPIKY HAIR **TALL**

WEARS MAKE-UP

You guessed it – it's another **trick question!** Beauty ideals can affect people in many different ways, but mostly they make us feel unhappy and like we don't fit in. Sometimes people can feel that low, they can become ill or decide to go to extreme lengths to change their appearance.

But why do these ideals even exist and who gets to decide on what it really means to be beautiful? The answer isn't completely straightforward, as some beauty ideals evolve over time and come from history. However, the biggest deciders of what is considered beautiful are **big brands**.

THE SECRETS
OF THE
BRANDS

Science tells us that when we feel low about ourselves and unhappy with our appearance, we are more likely to buy things to make ourselves feel better or to make us look more like we want to. Brands know this, which is why the models that they use in ads and the influencers and celebrities they work with look as close to the current beauty ideals as possible.

By **blasting you** with the image, it is only natural that you will compare yourself and feel pretty rubbish and therefore more likely that you will buy whatever it is they are trying to sell you. But guess what? Even the models and celebrities in the ads don't always feel comfortable or happy with how they look, because they too, are **under pressure.**

The list of beauty ideals is almost endless – here's a few of the pressures people face:

PRESSURES WE'RE ALL UNDER:

- Have clear skin
- Have white, straight teeth
- Be young
- Look like you work out
- Be photogenic
- Don't have anything that makes you unique (like a birth mark or something)
- Have little to no fat on your body

PRESSURES GUYS ARE UNDER:

- Be tall
- Have muscles
- Have facial hair
- Look sporty

PRESSURES GIRLS ARE UNDER:

- Have perfect hair
- Wear lots of make-up
- Have no body hair
- Be short
- Be skinny

Look at these lists – can you think of any products that brands might use in order to sell us something to obtain these ideals?

HERE ARE SOME EXAMPLES:

- **Clear skin:** could be used to sell cosmetics and make-up

- **Being muscly:** could be used to sell gym membership and protein powders

- **Being skinny:** could be used to sell diet aids

- **No body hair:** could be used to sell hair-removal products

If we all embraced how we **naturally** looked, do you think the beauty industry would exist? If it was considered "normal" for a woman to have as much body hair as a man, do you think hair removal products would exist? How about if guys weren't under so much pressure to be muscly, what would happen to the sales of protein bars and powders?

The truth is, big brands want us all to feel rubbish about ourselves because they know that when we feel low, we're more likely to spend cash to buy a product that claims to make us feel better. This makes them **a lot** of money.

But what can you do about it? Knowing the truth is a powerful start. It's important to know that the images you see of models and influencers on social media are almost always edited to make their appearance look even more **impossible**.

BODY SHAPES

The fact of the matter is, we were all born into a **different** body shape and there isn't a great deal that can be done about it.

A lot of people don't know that their body shape can't be changed, and so they spend a lot of time and money trying to fix something that isn't broken. Please always know that there is nothing broken about you. **You are unique and beautiful** and you do not need to change in order to try and chase impossible beauty ideals.

TEN TOP TIPS

My top ten tips for feeling comfortable in your own skin:

1 Whenever you find yourself talking or thinking negatively of your appearance, try to reframe it and focus on the things you like. The more we hear or say something, the more it feels true. **Be kind to yourself.** Putting yourself down in front of others only makes them feel like it's okay for them to do it too.

2 Remember that most of the photos you see online and in magazines are literally fake and edited. Nobody looks like the models in ad campaigns, **not even the models.**

3 Take filters with a pinch of salt. Sure, social media filters can make us feel a little better about ourselves by editing out blemishes and the things you dislike, but this can have a long-term, damaging impact on how you feel about and see yourself. If you're on social media, consider unfollowing the people you want to look like – every time you see their photo, it's just a reminder of the **unrealistic ideal you aspire to.**

Regularly remind yourself of the things you like about who you are – **not** how you look.

 Remember that people who make rude comments over how others look usually do it because they don't feel happy or confident within their own skin. If you find yourself thinking negatively of others and their appearance, try to shift your focus to finding something you like about them and know that we're all fighting our own private battles, so **please don't try to ever tear anybody down.**

 Delete the photo-editing apps on your phone and computer. **NOTHING GOOD EVER CAME FROM THEM. Literally, nothing.**

 Surround yourself with people who lift you up and make you feel good about yourself. Avoid friends who put you **under pressure** and who don't support you.

 If you find yourself looking in the mirror too much and **obsessing over your appearance**, try to shift your focus and reduce the amount of importance you place on it. There are many more important things about you, don't get caught up on one aspect.

Stop living for your diet. Enjoy your food. Be healthy and try to have a balanced diet, get some regular exercise but please don't obsess over it. Your weight does not represent how healthy you are. YOLO, so make the most of it.

Live your life for you. Define your own beauty ideals and try to ignore what other people think and say. Only insecure people feel the need to judge others, so be a rebel and rise above it.

Above all: if you're struggling with your appearance, know that you are definitely not alone and there is help available. Check out the useful resources page for some of the organizations you can speak to if you're feeling low right now.

You won't believe me when I say this but I guarantee in thirty years you'll look back at your photos and realize how **beautiful** you really were and if you spend the next twenty years bullying yourself, you'll regret it.

P.S. MICHELLE ELMAN

Here are some thoughts on being comfortable in your own skin, from

BODY CONFIDENCE COACH

My journey to **being comfortable in my skin** was a long and complicated one. It felt like as soon as I accepted one aspect of me, another **insecurity** would surface.

Eventually I actually found my power in realizing that even if I was the worst word I could think of – "ugly" – **ugly people are able to accomplish incredible things and live fulfilled lives**. So, I set about making my life more amazing outside of my appearance.

I quickly realized I've always been more than my beauty and actually when I made my life more full, it was then that I started realizing that "ugly" was a subjective word anyway and **no one has the power to decide that for you**.

YOUR OPINION OF **YOU** IS THE MOST IMPORTANT IN YOUR WORLD AND WHO'S TO SAY THEIR OPINION IS ANY MORE ACCURATE THAN YOURS?

A LETTER FROM LIAM

Oh my gosh, what a journey this has been. I wrote this book on and off for almost a year all over the world – Los Angeles, New York, London and Berlin. I really hope that you have enjoyed reading it as much as I enjoyed writing it.

The truth is: **stereotypes are all around us.** They're in the movies we watch, the music we listen to, the news and books we read and in the conversations we have. Every single day, we are learning new stereotypes, some good, and others not so good. It's clear from some of the weird and funny histories in this book that society has come a long way in improving, but there's still a lot to do.

I really believe that **you are the future** and you and everyone else growing up have the power to make the world a better place.

In this book we've focused mainly on **gender stereotypes** because that's where it all begins. It all starts with the first invisible box you're put inside and that box says either "girl" or "boy". We've looked at how the stereotypes can affect everything from how you feel about your body and how you deal with your emotions, to the kind of job you'll have when you're older and your hobbies and interests. We've also spoken a little about other types of stereotypes and how they can affect you and other people.

We can't forget that we all have stereotypes because our brains make them in order to build shortcuts. Not all stereotypes are bad, and there are useful activities throughout this book that you can do regularly in order to fix some of the bad stereotypes our brains create.

Growing up, I know that a book like this would have helped me a lot. I always felt different to everybody else and experienced some of the pressures that you are experiencing. Just knowing that I was normal and everything would turn out okay would have made so much difference to me.

So, if you're feeling like you're not normal or like you're under too much pressure, please take it from me that **everything will work out and you will find your happy.**

ULTIMATE TIPS

Let's finish with ten ultimate tips on how to be fearless in life. These are some of the lessons that I've learnt and I hope that they will help you too.

1 Not everybody you meet will be nice or want to see you happy. This is true for everybody, we all experience nasty people who want to hurt us. There is no way of hiding from them, but please remember that **only sad people try to make other people sad.** You are stronger than they are and please try not to take whatever it is they say personally. **You are not the problem.**

2 When you're feeling low, **use a positive mantra** to remind yourself of how fearless you really are. A mantra usually consists of three phrases that you repeat to yourself in order to battle the negative thoughts that you're thinking. I use positive mantras **A LOT!** If I'm nervous about talking to a large audience for example, I ask myself what three things are making me feel that way and build my mantra as the total opposite. For example, I may feel like I have nothing interesting to say and worried that I'll slip up my words, so my mantra would be something like: I am interesting, I am fearless and I am good at public speaking. There are loads of tips online about mantras, so if you're still unsure, Google is your friend!

3 **Keep a gratitude diary** and at the end of each day, write down three things that you are grateful for and three things that you did, however big or small, that were brave and fearless. My gratitude journal last night says I was grateful for my family, good music and the birds in my garden. Three brave things that I did were going to a new gym, seeing my dentist and cooking a new recipe. Some days you'll find it easy to think of things to write, other days it may feel like a struggle – but stick at it. It's a daily reminder of how many positive things you have in your life and how fearless you really are. Whenever you're feeling a bit meh, it's there for you as a reminder.

4 **Find your tribe** and know a good friend from a bad one. A good friend is somebody who accepts you and makes you feel good about yourself. A bad friend is somebody that makes you feel like you need to do something you don't want to in order to impress them and who pulls you down. Find people who are like you and who make you feel good, and stop wasting your time trying to please people who wouldn't give you much of theirs.

5 Try new things regularly and often and once you've found things that give you your flow, make sure you do them at least a few times a week.

6 **Remember that good and bad things happen to us all** and that negative emotions are normal, healthy and okay. **If you need to cry, cry.** If you need to vent, vent. Don't let anyone make you think that it isn't okay to let it all out. Bottling up your emotions will only make things worse. If you're feeling low all the time, it may be a sign that there's something bigger going on and it might be a good idea to speak to your family doctor.

7 Know that **you are unique** and different from everybody else. You are special and people love and care about you. We all feel lonely and low sometimes, but just because you have negative thoughts about yourself or people make mean comments, doesn't make it true. You are never alone and there are so many people out there who have been through what you're going through and many others going through the same thing. Talk whenever you feel like you need to get something off your chest or get advice, check out some of the great places you can find support in the Useful Resources section.

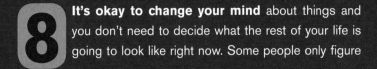

8 **It's okay to change your mind** about things and you don't need to decide what the rest of your life is going to look like right now. Some people only figure out what they want to do when they're older, when they are … older! And that's okay. Be in the moment and follow the subjects you most enjoy at school. Have an open mind and be willing to try new things. I believe that everything happens for a reason and you'll get to the place you're supposed to.

9 **Remember** that life is a constant journey of **self-improvement** and discovery. You'll never stop learning new things about yourself and the world around you, so be open to change and never stop your journey of trying to become a better person.

10 **Spend time in the moment** instead of taking photos of the moment. I don't know about you, but most of the pics I take I never even use anyway. Put your phone down, be in control of it and not the other way around. Science literally tells us that it's good to be with other people and healthy to hug, so turn off your notifications and look at the world around you.

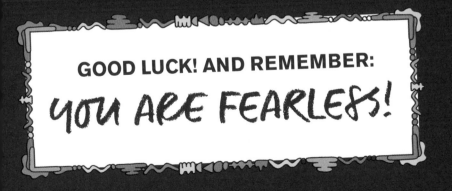

GOOD LUCK! AND REMEMBER:

YOU ARE FEARLESS!

GLOSSARY

A

adaptive behaviour when we change behaviour to fit in with a certain situation

agender to be "agender" is to not have a gender identity

B

beauty ideals the pressures that we're all put under to look a certain way

bias liking something or someone without showing fairness

breadwinner the person who earns the most money in a family

D

DNA 'deoxyribonucleic acid', the material that carries all the information about a living thing

F

flow when you find something that you enjoy so much that it completely takes over your mind

G

gender identity your personal sense of gender that may or may not match the sex assigned to you at birth

H

hard drive a computer's
storage device

hormones chemicals that tell
your body parts to do things

M

manual labour another
name for physical work

meditate to rest quietly and
calm your mind down

N

non-binary gender any gender
identity that isn't male or female

S

social enterprise a business
that tries to change the
world for the better

stereotype a widely believed
idea of a person or thing

stress a reaction to a
pressure or a threat

subjective when a viewpoint
is based on personal opinion

T

transgender a transgender
person is someone whose gender
identity doesn't match the sex
they were assigned at birth

U

unconscious bias when our
brains decide if we like or dislike
somebody without us even
being aware of the decision

USEFUL RESOURCES

WHERE TO GET HELP

A problem shared is a problem halved … that's my motto!
Sometimes we all need a little advice and someone to listen to us! Here are some of the places you can turn to for support.

DITCH THE LABEL

You can chat to the Ditch the Label mentors online about most things covered in this book. They've also got tons of useful guides and a really boss Instagram for a daily dose of positivity. Examples of the things you can talk to them about include bullying, cyberbullying, mental health, relationships, stereotypes, gender, sexuality and ways to boost your confidence. **Free for everybody and mainly for people below 25.**
www.ditchthelabel.org

CHILDLINE

You can call Childline for advice on a wide range of issues such as: problems at home, relationships, schoolwork and mental health. **You can either call them for free on 0800 11 11 or visit their website** for more information.
www.childline.org.uk

YOUNG MINDS

These folks have some **pretty cool resources** when it comes to looking after your mental health. They also do some really awesome work at raising awareness and encouraging people to talk more about their mental health.

www.youngminds.org.uk

MIND

If you're worried about your mental health or feel like you'd benefit from learning more, MIND is a great charity with loads of tips and advice on their website. **They can help with things like depression, anxiety and loneliness.**

www.mind.org.uk

INDEX